Dear Parent:

Congratulations! Your child is taking the first steps on an exciting journey. The destination? Independent reading!

STEP INTO READING® will help your child get there. The program offers books at five levels that accompany children from their first attempts at reading to reading success. Each step includes fun stories, fiction and nonfiction, and colorful art. There are also Step into Reading Sticker Books, Step into Reading Math Readers, and Step into Reading Phonics Readers— a complete literacy program with something to interest every child.

Learning to Read, Step by Step!

Ready to Read Preschool–Kindergarten
• big type and easy words • rhyme and rhythm • picture clues
For children who know the alphabet and are eager to begin reading.

Reading with Help Preschool–Grade 1
• basic vocabulary • short sentences • simple stories
For children who recognize familiar words and sound out new words with help.

Reading on Your Own Grades 1–3
• engaging characters • easy-to-follow plots • popular topics
For children who are ready to read on their own.

Reading Paragraphs Grades 2–3
• challenging vocabulary • short paragraphs • exciting stories
For newly independent readers who read simple sentences with confidence.

Ready for Chapters Grades 2–4
• chapters • longer paragraphs • full-color art
For children who want to take the plunge into chapter books but still like colorful pictures.

STEP INTO READING® is designed to give every child a successful reading experience. The grade levels are only guides. Children can progress through the steps at their own speed, developing confidence in their reading, no matter what their grade.

Remember, a lifetime love of reading starts with a single step!

For Tim and Lois Wilson—S.R.R.

*To my son, Parks, and daughter, Wynn, with thanks
to the University of Washington Marine Laboratories,
the students of Friday Harbor Elementary School
and the mariners of the Port of Friday Harbor—B.B.*

*With grateful acknowledgment to
Clyde F. E. Roper, Ph.D., zoologist,
National Museum of Natural History,
and Jennifer Fiegel, educational specialist
at the National Aquarium in Baltimore.*

Photo credits:
pp. 20, 21, 33, 39, 44, 45: © I. H. Roper;
p. 29: © Earl & Nazima Kowall/CORBIS;
p. 37: © C.F.E. Roper; p. 38: © *The Evening Post,*
Wellington, N.Z.; p. 41: © Tasmanian Museum & Art Gallery.

www.stepintoreading.com

Educators and librarians, for a variety of teaching tools, visit us at
www.randomhouse.com/teachers

Library of Congress Cataloging-in-Publication Data
Redmond, Shirley Raye.
Tentacles! : tales of the giant squid / by Shirley Raye Redmond ; illustrated by Bryn Barnard.
p.   cm. — (Step into reading. A step 3 book)
SUMMARY: Describes some of the exaggerated stories that have been told about giant squids
and also what scientists have learned about their real physical characteristics and behavior.
ISBN 0-375-81307-1 (trade) — ISBN 0-375-91307-6 (lib. bdg.)
1. Giant squids—Juvenile literature. [1. Giant squids. 2. Squids.] I. Barnard, Bryn, ill.
II. Title. III. Series: Step into reading. Step 3 book. QL430.3.A73 R43 2003 594'.58—dc21
2002010238

Printed in the United States of America First Edition 10 9 8 7 6 5 4 3 2 1

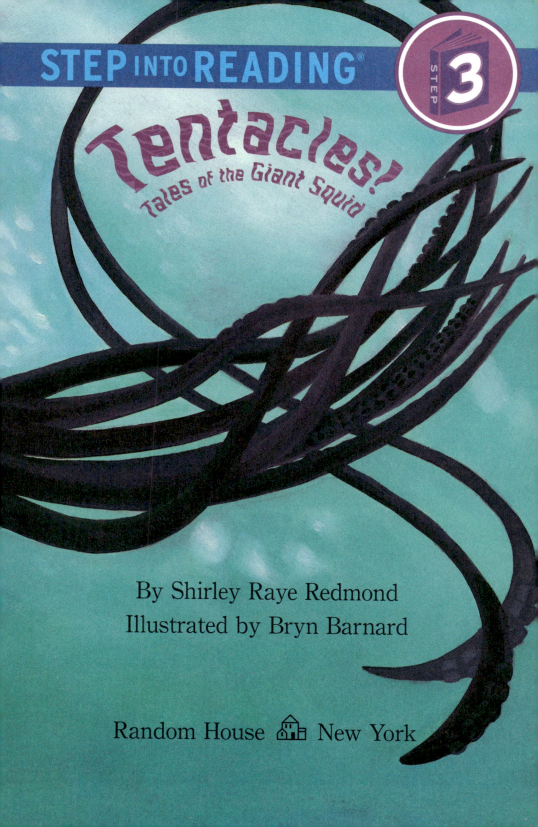

STEP INTO READING®

STEP 3

Tentacles!
Tales of the Giant Squid

By Shirley Raye Redmond

Illustrated by Bryn Barnard

Random House 🏠 New York

The giant squid is a
creature of mystery.
Few people have ever seen
this monster of the deep.
No one has seen it
alive and healthy
in its home.

For a long time,
people thought
the giant squid
was a myth.
Sailors told
scary tales about it.

They said
the squid's huge eyes
could hypnotize people.

They told stories
of the giant squid
chasing sailing ships.
They said it could
stretch its arms
around a ship.
Then it could
pull the ship
down into the sea.

But the giant squid
is not a myth.
The giant squid is *real*.
In the 1930s,
a magazine reported
that a giant squid
attacked an oil freighter.

The story said the squid
tried to wrap its arms
around the freighter.
But it could not get
a firm grip.

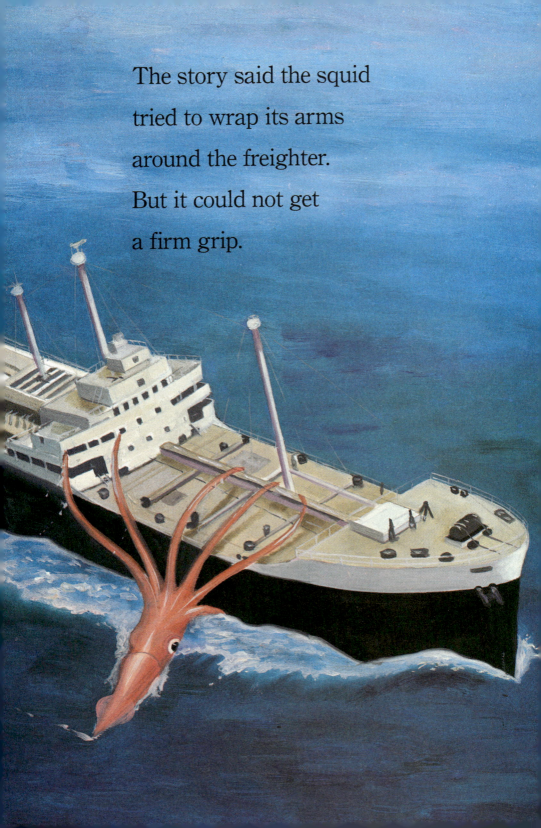

The squid slid off.

It was killed

by the ship's propellers.

Some giant squid stories
are even more deadly.
During World War II,
British sailors said
a giant squid pulled
a man overboard.
He was never seen again.

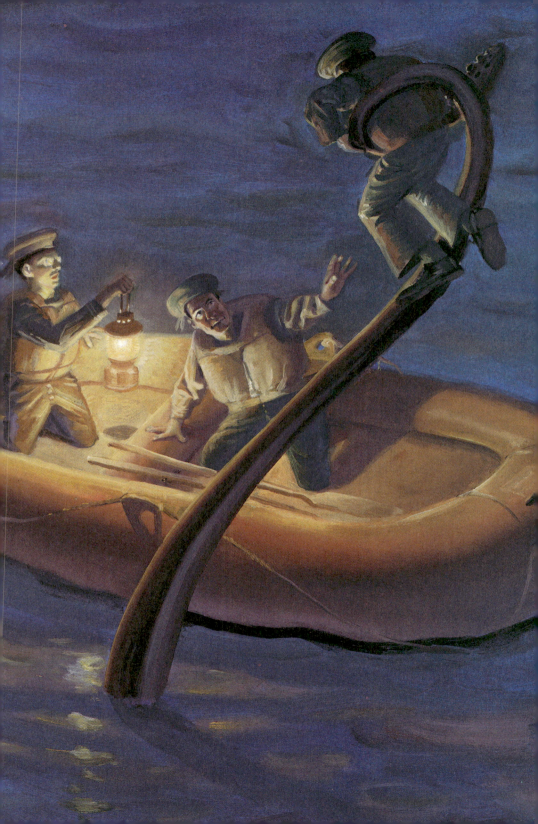

In the 1960s,
lighthouse keepers
said a giant squid
battled a baby whale—
and won!

Could these stories be true?

17

Scientists today say no.
We do not know much
about the giant squid.
But we do know
that it is not
as strong as a whale.

We also know

that the giant squid

lives deep in the ocean.

It only comes to the surface

when it is dead or dying.

Could a sick squid

attack a giant ship?

What do *you* think?

People tell stories
to explain things
they do not understand.
Scientists are trying
to understand the giant squid.
That will help them
figure out what is real—
and what is not.

For instance,
some people call
the giant squid
a "devilfish."
But it is not a fish at all.
It is a mollusk.
(Say MAH-lusk.)
Mollusks have
soft, slippery bodies.
They do not have backbones.

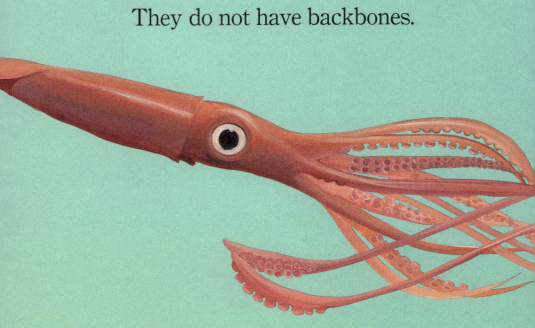

Octopuses, snails, and clams
are mollusks, too.

octopus

snail

clam

The giant squid is
the biggest mollusk.
Its eyes are the largest
of any living creature
on Earth.
These eyes are as big
as a human head!

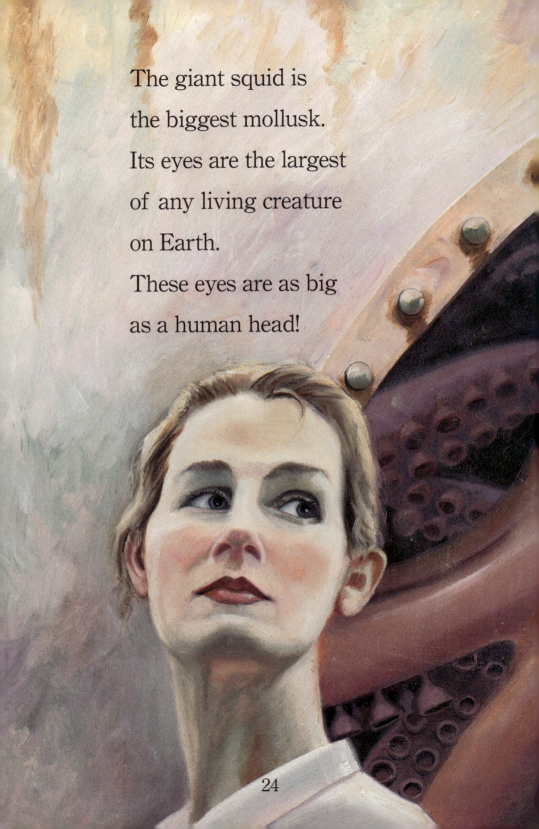

The giant squid has
two long tentacles
and eight arms.
If a giant squid
were stretched out
on a baseball field,
it would reach
from home plate
to the pitcher's mound.

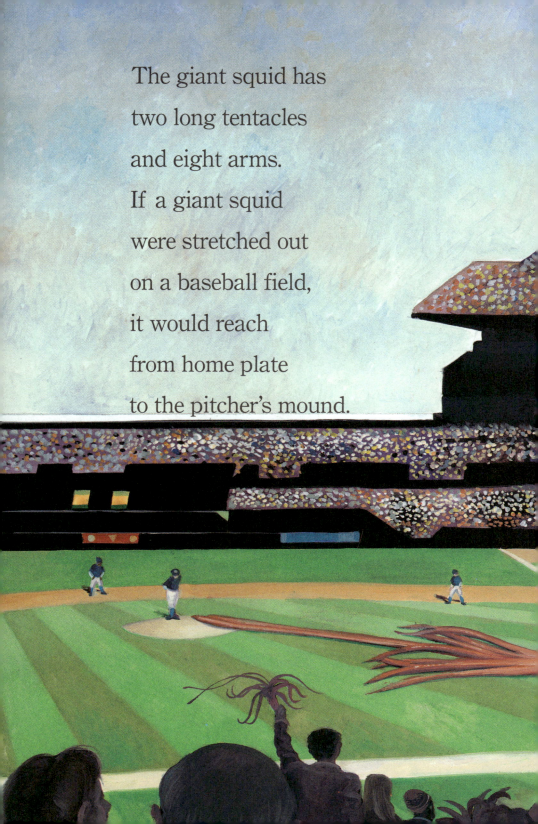

Not all squids
are giants, though.
Some are so small
they could swim
in a cereal bowl.

Many people eat
small squid.
Squid can be served
fried or steamed.
Some like them
in a salad or on a stick.

Large or small,

a squid's body

is shaped like a tube.

Its mouth looks

like a parrot's beak.

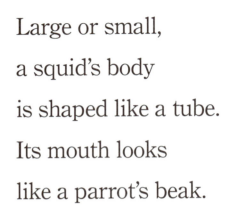

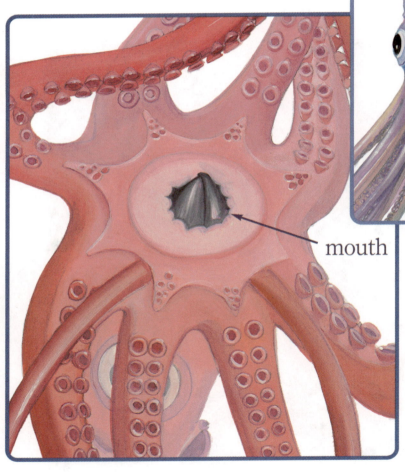

mouth

A squid's beak
is strong.
A giant squid
could break a wooden oar
in one bite.
Snap!

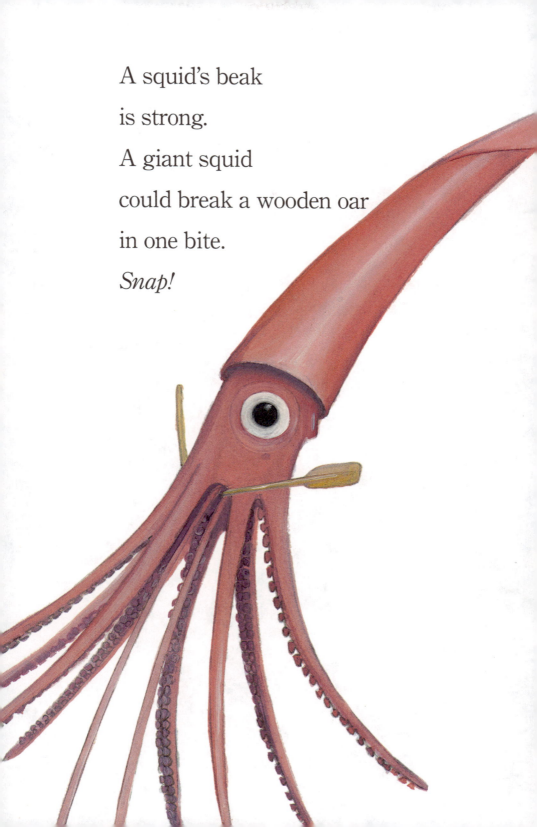

The giant squid does not
eat oars, though.
The giant squid eats fish.
This giant squid's tentacles
reach out to catch a fish.

32

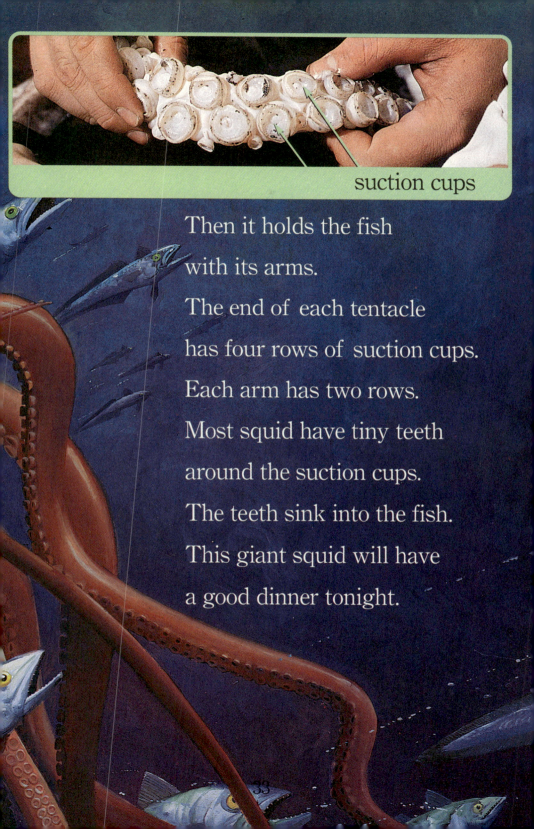

suction cups

Then it holds the fish
with its arms.
The end of each tentacle
has four rows of suction cups.
Each arm has two rows.
Most squid have tiny teeth
around the suction cups.
The teeth sink into the fish.
This giant squid will have
a good dinner tonight.

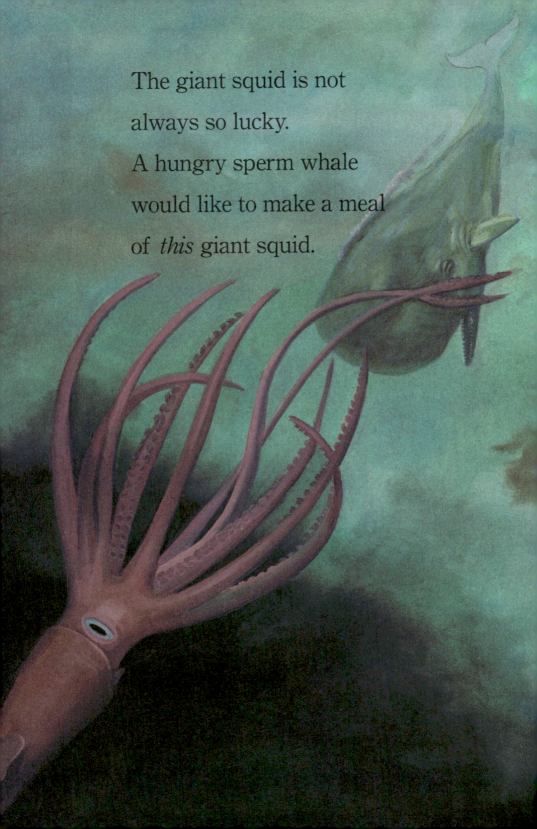

The giant squid is not
always so lucky.
A hungry sperm whale
would like to make a meal
of *this* giant squid.

Some types of squid
have a secret weapon.
It is an ink sac.
When the squid is scared,
it squirts the ink.
The inky water
distracts the attacker.
The squid can escape.
Does the giant squid
squirt ink?

No one knows.
But we do know
that the giant squid
does not give up
without a fight.

See the round scars
on this whale's skin?
The suction cups
of a giant squid
made those scars.

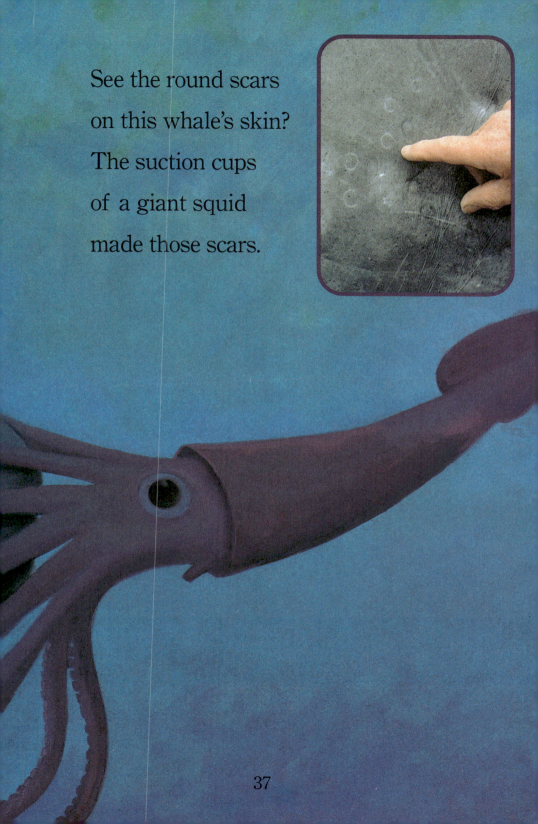

How do scientists know
all this about the giant squid?
They know because
dead squids wash up
on beaches around the world.

Scientists study
these dead giants.
The biggest one
ever discovered
weighed almost 1,000 pounds.
This squid weighs 300 pounds.
It is only a teenager!

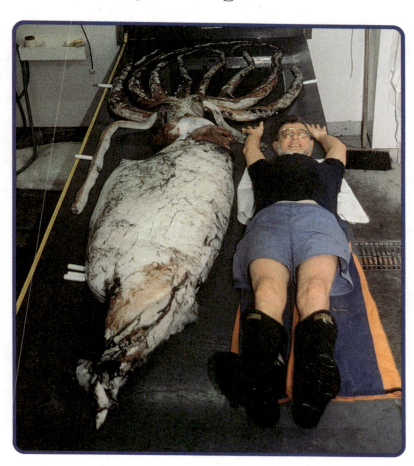

In 1996,
fishermen snagged
three dead giants
near New Zealand.
The squids' long arms
were almost as thick as
a man's thigh.

In 2002,

another dead squid washed up

on a beach in Australia.

Scientists came to see it.

Schoolchildren came

to see it, too.

Now scientists are trying
to find a giant squid—alive!
They are doing this
by tracking sperm whales.

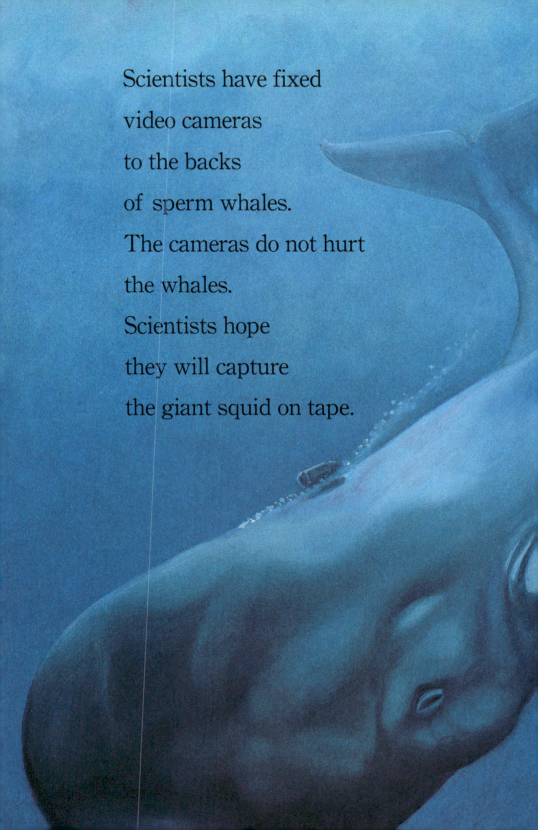

Scientists have fixed
video cameras
to the backs
of sperm whales.
The cameras do not hurt
the whales.
Scientists hope
they will capture
the giant squid on tape.

This scientist is also
searching with *Deep Rover*.
Deep Rover is a
one-person submarine.

How deep can
a giant squid swim?
How big can it grow?
How long does it live?
These are all questions
scientists cannot answer yet.
But they are working hard
to find out.

Maybe someone like you
will grow up and unlock
the secrets of the giant squid.

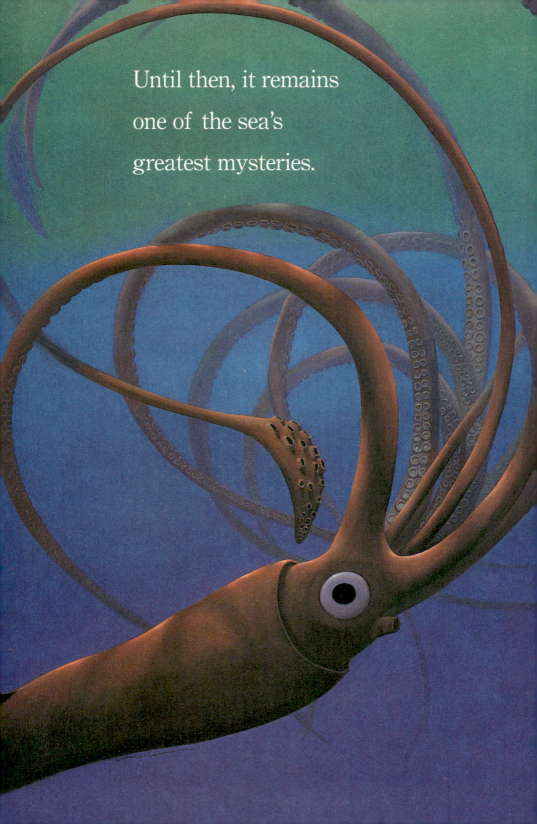

Until then, it remains
one of the sea's
greatest mysteries.